M000191098

When Nobody Brings You An Apple

Over 101 Proverbs and Quotes To Encourage
and Inspire Your Favorite Teachers,
Principals, Support Staff,
and School Administrators

Volume One

Joseph "Mr. B." Butts

Apple Hearts Media
Clarkston, Georgia

When Nobody Brings You An Apple

Over 101 Proverbs and Quotes To Encourage and
Inspire Your Favorite Teachers, Principals,
Support Staff, and School Administrators

Volume One

by Joseph "Mr. B" Butts

Published by:

Apple Hearts Media
Atlanta, Georgia

Visit our website at **www.applehearts.com**

**Copyright © 2012 by Joseph Butts. All Rights
Reserved.**

**No part of this book may be reproduced or transmitted in
any form or by any means, electronic or mechanical,
including photocopying, recording or by any information
storage and retrieval system without written permission
from the author, except for the inclusion of brief quotations
in critical articles or reviews.**

Special Dedication

This book is dedicated to teachers and mothers (our first teachers).

Teachers are the unsung heroes of our nation, our society, and our world as we know it. They are the people that care, without being cared for. They love without sometimes being loved in return. And most give without any thought of receiving.

This book is for you.

Acknowledgments

This book is dedicated to my mother, Carrie Butts, who gave me all that she had to give and then gave what she didn't have to give. You are the original teacher that instilled in me the confidence to know that I could do anything that I put my mind to do. I love you.

This book is dedicated to all of my teachers from first grade up through college. And to the little schools that planted big dreams into the minds of its children and students: Miami Union Academy and Oakwood College (now Oakwood University).

A special dedication to the people that quietly support the teachers, professors, schools, colleges, universities, administrators, and students: the support staff.

To the cafeteria workers, food services employees, janitors, custodial workers, groundskeepers, nurses, campus security, counselors, librarians, media specialists, secretaries, administrative assistants, front desk assistants, volunteers, PTA members, and every one else that give of their time and energy so that the lives of children can be enriched. Teachers may be the sun but you are the stars.

To the principals, assistant principals, and administrators. You are the guiding lights that lead.

To all of "my" students in Fulton county: *Thank you for teaching me what teaching is all about.*

jmb

Table of Contents

Preface

This book was compiled and written to encourage and inspire our nation's teachers. You (they) are truly the backbone of our society whether society admits it or not.

Teaching can be a very lonely profession at times. Even though you are constantly around children all day there are times when you can feel like you're the only person in the world. You work in isolation from your peers for most of the day, and the burdens of the world inside the classroom are solely on your shoulders.

There is a great satisfaction. But there are many times that your efforts go unrewarded. And often, the fruits of your labor are delayed until times when you may or may not see them. You truly have to work by faith knowing that the seeds that you plant today will bring an abundant harvest in the future. And they do!

This book is a pick-me-up for those days when you wonder if it is really all worth it. It is!

Just think back in time to a teacher or mentor that made a difference in your life. They may not have known the full affect that they were having on you, but because of them you are a better person today.

This is the same experience that you can bring to the life of a child or student today. ***"Keep on keeping on"***.

Students and children pay attention. They may act like they don't but they really do. Keep planting the seeds because you never know which ones will rise to the sun. And most of them do. But you already know this.

We can do all things through Christ when we depend on His strength.

How to use this book

If you really want to get the most out of this book, I suggest that you **use it as a journal**. Write your thoughts in the spaces after each quote or proverb, and then try to apply the thought to different situations in your life.

Really take ownership of this book by marking in it and writing notes throughout it.

You can even keep this as a memento to **pass along your wisdom** to your children or grandchildren. If you come across something that really speaks to your heart, take the time to share it with others. Give them the benefit of your newly acquired insights.

To my fellow teachers, you should **keep this book on your desk and take a minute or two to read from it throughout the day**. Parents can also read bits and pieces in between their daily tasks.

The more you read and reread from this book, the deeper will become your understanding of its wisdom.

Enjoy.

*(Please share your thoughts with me by sending an email to **mythoughts@applehearts.com**)*

My First Day In A Classroom
(The following was taken from my website.)

Dear Friends, Family and Visitors,

It is with great joy and pleasure that I announce to you the publishing of my first book.

As some of you may know, I have been living in Atlanta for the past several years. You may also know that after being in Atlanta for a few years I quit my "big-time" corporate job and started my own business; a graphic art and web design company.

This turned out to be a BIG MISTAKE!

Starting my own business wasn't the mistake. Quitting my job without having a STEADY source of income was the mistake! (If you ever decide to start your own business, I would suggest that you have a nice stash of cash in the bank, or, have a steady stream of clients or orders for your product before you decide to go it alone. BUT YOU CAN DO IT!)

I started my company and I was out on my own. It was a long-time dream come true. I was ready to take on the world and do battle with "the competition".

Well, before I knew it, the reality of having "my own " business set in. Times got HARD! Everyday I was making dozens of calls to prospective clients but the work was just not coming in like I had expected it to.

Everyone knew that the Internet was "going to be the future" but no one I contacted wanted to invest in having their own website created (this was way back yonder in 2000- early 2001). And not many people saw the need of having a visual representation, or logo, for their business.

And what was worse is that a few months after I quit my job, our nation was attacked by terrorists on September 11. (Talk about my bad timing.)

That's when things got really TOUGH!

Most people were not thinking about having artwork or web design done for their business. They were more concerned with whether or not someone was going to bomb their children's school, or attack the local strip mall down the street. It was as if someone had turned off the water hose that spurted out new business.

No one was spending on ANYTHING!

And as for me, things went from bad to worse. My lights got cut off during this time, my car broke down and needed repair, and my meals began to consist of Ramen noodles with fried tomatoes, and powdered milk. (Thank God for Ramen noodles!)

It was about this time that one of my uncles suggested that I look into substitute teaching with a local school system. I had heard someone mention the idea before but I never really gave it that much thought. I found out that by working part-time as a substitute teacher, I could set my own schedule, earn some extra money, and still work on building my business.

Well by that time my meals were starting to consist of just fried tomatoes (seasoned with salt, pepper, and oregano) and powdered milk. The lights were back on but I didn't know for how long (every month those scoundrels at Georgia Power sent a new electric bill).

Things were tight and if I didn't do something fast they were going to get even tighter.

The more I thought about it the more substitute teaching seemed like a good idea. My mother had even suggested that I would be a good candidate for teaching because of my patience and easy going nature. I wasn't too sure about that, but I thought that I could at least give it a try.

Education has always been held in high esteem in my family. And I had real positive memories of my own teachers and school experiences. I also had been praying and I knew that God would lead me to the right opportunities. And deep down inside I felt like this was one.

So that was it. I made up my mind that I would do it!

I researched the surrounding counties and decided that I'd try Fulton county. I went to the main office for Fulton County Schools and filled out an application.

I was accepted and given a date for substitute teacher orientation. The orientation would be given during a one day workshop that would include training, details about expectations, and other information relating to the job.

The workshop was conducted by a retired seasoned veteran of the educational system, Dr. Lynch, and two members from Substitute Services from the Fulton County School system, Linda Coffey and Nancy O'Barr.

The room was filled with enthusiastic but anxiously hesitant people that were ready to march into classrooms and serve students with warm-hearted vigor. The workshop was part motivation, part information, and part illumination.

Near the close of the workshop we were each given a sheet of paper that had a list of classes and grade levels that we would be willing to work with. The sheet had areas such as Reading, Social Studies, Band, Language Arts, Gifted, Elementary, Middle Grades, High School, and a whole lot of others.

The possibilities seemed to offer unknown challenges and adventures. I chose several subjects that I thought I could be of best service to the students. And I chose all three grade levels: Elementary, Middle, and High schools.

I turned my sheet in, said good bye to the facilitators, and then left to go back home.

The workshop happened during the Christmas holiday break or sometime close to it. So it would be about two weeks before I actually got my first official classroom assignment.

I waited with anticipation not really knowing what to expect. "Would the kids like me?", "Would I like them?", "Would I be in the classrooms alone or would I have an assistant?" These were all questions that were racing through my head while I "waited for the bell".

Well, before I knew it the holidays were over and students were getting ready to go back to school.

The moment of truth was drawing closer.

I can remember it almost like it was yesterday! It was about two days after school had started back and my telephone rang. I didn't recognize the number on the caller I.D. screen and I knew that it must be CASE, the automated phone system that would be alerting me to available classroom assignments.

I hesitated for a moment, not knowing if I really wanted to answer the call. Doubts began to rush through my mind again. But something inside of me seemed to push me to answer it.

"Hello?"

There was a short pause and then a recorded voice came through the line. A voice that I would hear dozens and dozens more times in the upcoming years.

"This is Fulton County CASE, the Central Assignment for Substitute Employees." The voice went on to ask me for my identification number and PIN.

After I entered my information into the phone the voice then gave a description of the assignment that I was being offered to take.

My very first assignment, if I chose to take it, would be a kindergarten class at Harriet Tubman Elementary school. How fitting. I knew that God had been watching over me throughout this whole process and I believe that

He knew exactly what I needed to introduce me to the world of teaching.

I accepted the assignment for the next day and feverishly began to prepare myself. I got my clothes ready, my "Sub Pack"* ready, and my lunch for the day ready. I was set.

At least almost. I also had to find out what buses would take me by the school. My car was still "broke" and so was I. I would need to ride the bus until I was able to get my car back on the road.

That night I hardly slept a wink. My mind was racing a 'mile-a-minute' with more questions. "What would the day hold?", "How would the students act?", and "What if I overslept and missed the bus?"

Before I realized it I had dozed off. But just as suddenly the alarm clock began to ring letting me know that it was time to get up and get ready for school. My first day at school!

I got up and had a short morning devotional which consisted of reading from the Bible, prayer, and another short reading. I then got dressed, ate a small breakfast, and was out the door.

It turned out that I would need to catch a bus, the "train" (MARTA), and another bus to get to the school. This was fine with me because I wouldn't have to fight the Atlanta traffic and I could relax and read on the trip there and back. (It's been found that Atlantans have one of the longest commutes to work in the United States.)

I arrived at the school right on time. As I walked through the halls I was met with bright smiles and warm hellos. I must have looked lost because someone approached me and asked if I was looking for the front office.

They volunteered to show me and I was soon at the front desk signing in. (I would later come to learn that it wasn't just that I looked lost, but that most teachers know when other teachers will be out for the day. And so if they see a new face they know that in most cases it's either a substitute teacher coming for an assignment, or a parent of one of the students.)

After I signed in I was shown to the classroom and given the teacher's lesson plans for the day.

The students had not yet started coming into the classroom and so I still had a little time to mentally prepare myself for the job-at-hand. A minute or so later the teacher's assistant came into the room and introduced herself.

She told me that she would be back and forth between classrooms and if I needed anything I could just let her know.

I thought to myself that I needed something alright. I needed her to stay in the classroom with me just in case there was some type of "uprising"!

It was right about this time that one-by-one the students began to come into the room. I said a short prayer to myself asking God for wisdom and then greeted each student with a big smile and a cheery "Good morning".

Most of the students followed the same routine. They would enter the classroom stopping just inside the door, offer a hesitant "Good morning", and then look around wide-eyed for their teacher. Then they would come in, put up their books and coats, sit down, and immediately lock their eyes on me.

You could almost hear their thoughts. "Who is this man?...And why is he here?...And where is my teacher?...And why is he looking at me like that?"

Most of the students were now seated at their tables and the classroom was abuzz with whispering and speculation.

Finally, one of the students stood up and walked up to the front of the class where the assistant and I were standing. I took it that this was the class "spokesperson". As he walked up to the front the room got so quiet you could have heard a pin drop. The only sounds coming from the room was the occasional giggle or "shhhhhhhh" that originated from the small sea of faces.

My heart started pounding. This would be my first "showdown".

I watched as this "little person" that barely reached my waist came up to me with all boldness and intensity of purpose, look me directly in the eye, and then while trying to hold back a "snaggatooth" smile asked the most profound question that his innocent mind had probably ever pondered.

"Are you our NEW teacher?", he asked me, with his eyes so wide that they looked like they were going to pop out of their sockets.

The innocence and sincerity of the question almost brought tears to my eyes. I looked at "my" assistant, as she gave me an encouraging nod, and then I stooped down to eye-level with the trusting eyes that had asked me the question. I knew that even though the question had come from only one mouth, the answer was being anticipated by dozens of little ears.

"No. I'm not your NEW teacher. I'm just your teacher for TODAY", I said.

"Oh", he replied.

And with that settled the "spokesperson" turned around and walked contentedly back to his seat.

I was then officially introduced to the class and once again the class was abuzz. Questions and commentary started coming from everywhere. "Will you take us out to recess?", "Are you nice?", "Do you have any children?", "Can I be your helper for the day?", "No, I want to be his helper!", "You can't be the helper you got in trouble yesterday!", "So what!!!! He can pick anybody he wants to pick!"

"EXCUSE ME!", I said in a loud and booming "teacherly" voice.

The room immediately got quiet again. The whole class was now looking up and watching me intensely with a mixture of wonder and fear.

"Now I KNOW that your teacher doesn't just let everyone speak at one time. Now does she?", I asked while allowing my voice to take on a more gentler tone.

"Noooooooooo", came back the singsong chorus from the children.

"And I KNOW that everyone knows that they're suppose to raise their hand and wait for permission to speak. Right?", I asked.

"Yeeeeeeeeess", the children said in an off-key unison.

"Alright", I began. "We're going to have a good day today. But, I need everyone to remember how we're suppose to act in the classroom, do your best work, and then maybe we can go outside for recess." And then for good measure I added, "But only if you're good!"

Excitement broke out once again as the thought of recess flowed through the children's minds.

"He IS nice! He IS nice!", I heard echo around the room.

But this time instead of trying to curb their enthusiasm, I secretly joined in.

That day was the beginning of a new learning experience for me. An experience that would not just be about teaching, or about education, or just about students. But an experience that was a mixture of the three. An experience that would far exceed the sum of its parts.

It was a new type of awareness about the power of faith. A sudden enlightenment about the value and potential of every student. A new awe and appreciation for the worth of teachers.

That experience began an awakening in me to the fact that everyone can make a difference in this world if they are only willing to serve others and give of themselves unselfishly.

And that's what most teachers do.

And it's for them that I wrote this book, "When Nobody Brings You An Apple".

My first day in the classroom turned out to be a good one. And I have since gone on to teach many other classes. And with each new experience my appreciation for teachers has deepened and grown fonder.

Teachers are truly the hidden gems of our society.

I say "hidden" gems because being a teacher is a very unique experience. Teachers literally have a part in shaping the future. Their experience is one similar to that of a planter or farmer. They plant seeds in the minds of students and then must wait to see what fruit their labors will bring.

Teachers often work with no recognition of their efforts until something goes wrong. And then when something does go wrong they receive a disproportionate amount of the blame.

But they still stay the course day-in and day-out.

They plant good seed and continue to have faith in the future harvest.

That's the purpose of this book. To plant positive seeds in the minds of teachers and others that work with, and care for children.

Seeds that will encourage them to continue to give of themselves even though they may not always immediately see the results of their efforts.

Seeds that will inspire teachers to continue to have faith in the possibilities of the future.

Seeds that will bring forth a positive harvest in their minds "when nobody brings them an apple".

This book is to be used as a soothing balm on those days that seem like nothing is going right, and nobody seems to care. For those days when it seems like every student is on their "worst" behavior and still need the BEST from you.

This book is filled with words of wisdom that have been passed through the hands of time. Words that have brought encouragement and inspiration to untold numbers.

"When Nobody Brings You An Apple" is for those days...when nobody brings you an apple!

Sincerely Yours,
Joseph "Mr. B" Butts

*Sub Pack: A small supply of pencils, crayons, worksheets, and other classroom items that you might need throughout a regular day in the classroom. The contents are often dictated by the grade level that you are assigned.

Acceptance

1. **"He who does not know one thing knows another." (Kenyan)**

Age

2. "Age is honorable and youth is noble." (Irish)

3. "A new broom sweeps clean, but the old brush knows all the corners." (Irish)

Attitude

4."Open your door to a good day and prepare yourself for a bad one." (from Moon Over Morocco)

5. "Keep a green tree in your heart and perhaps a singing bird will come." (Chinese)

6. "Anticipate the good so that you may enjoy it."

Books

7. **"A book is like a garden carried in the pocket." (Arab)**

Children

8. "A child is what you put into him."

9. "Children are the reward of life." (Zaire)

10. "Small children give you headache; big children heartache." (Russian)

11. "Remember that your children are not your own, but are lent to you by the Creator." (Mohawk)

Classrooms

12. **"The cattle is as good as the pasture in which it grazes." (Ethiopia)**

Community

13. **"It takes a whole village to raise a child."**
(Yoruba)

Confidence

14. **"You must act as if it is impossible to fail." (Ashanti)**

Consequences

15. **"When the roots of a tree begin to decay, it spreads death to the branches."**

Constraint

16. **"Who begins too much accomplishes little."**

Cooperation

17. "When spider webs
unite, they can
tie up a lion."
(Ethiopia)

18. "When the right hand
washes the left hand
and the left hand washes
the right hand,
both hands become
clean."

Courage

19. "If you're not living on the edge, you're taking up too much room."

20. "Courage is the father of success."

Criticism

21. "Any fool can criticize, condemn, and complain, and most fools do." (Benjamin Franklin)

22. "Criticism is easy but it does not create."

Crying

23. "Don't be afraid to cry. It will free your mind of sorrowful thoughts." (Hopi)

24. "The soul would have no rainbow if the eye had no tears." (Native American)

Dedication

25. "An oil lamp
feels proud to give light
even though it
wears itself away."

26. "Nothing is impossible
to a willing heart."
(John Heywood)

27. "We will water the thorn
for the sake of the rose."
(Kanem)

Destiny

28. "An ant hill that is destined to become a giant ant hill will definitely become one, no matter how many times it is destroyed by elephants."

29. "It doesn't take time to change one's destiny." (Kashmiri)

30. **"If you are on a road to nowhere, find another road." (Ashanti)**

Discretion

31. **"It is better to conceal one's knowledge than to reveal one's ignorance." (Spanish)**

Enemies

32. **"He who cannot agree with his enemies is controlled by them."**
(Chinese)

Faith

33. **"Faith is the bird that sings when the dawn is still dark."**
(Tagore)

34. **"It is not because things are difficult that we do not dare, it is because we do not dare that they are difficult."**
(Lucius Seneca)

Family

35. "The ruin of a nation
begins in the homes
of its people."
(Ashanti)

36. "It is the habit
that a child
forms at home,
that follows them
to their marriage."

Fear

**37. "Be not afraid
of going slowly;
be afraid only
of standing still."
(Chinese)**

Fools

38. "The best way to convince a fool that he is wrong is to let him have his own way." (Josh Billings)

39. "By the time the fool has learned the game, the players have dispersed."

Friends

40. **"A friend is someone you share the path with."**
(Nilotic)

Gentleness

41. **"Never cut what can be untied."**
(Portuguese)

God

42. **"God conceals himself from the mind of man, but reveals himself to his heart."**

Gossip

43. **"A rumor goes in one ear and out many mouths." (Chinese)**

Gratitude

44. "Get down on your knees and thank God you're still on your feet." (Irish)

45. "By being grateful, a man makes himself deserving of yet another kindness."

Happiness

46. "**Dance as if no one's watching, sing as if no one's listening, and live everyday as if it were your last.**"
(Irish)

Hate

47. **"Without knowing a person we must not hate him."**

48. **"There is no medicine to cure hatred."**
(Ashanti)

Honesty

49. "Honesty is
the best policy."
(English)

50. "A lie travels round the
world while truth is
putting her boots on."
(French)

51. "A clear conscience is a
soft pillow."
(German)

52. "Speak the truth, but leave immediately after." (Slovenian)

Hope

53. **"Hope is the pillar of the world."**
(Kanuri)

54. **"No matter how long the winter, spring is sure to follow."**
(Guinea)

55. **"No matter how long the night, the day is sure to come."**

56. **"The darkest hour is that before the dawn."**
(English)

Humility

57. **"He who would climb
the ladder
must begin at
the bottom."
(English)**

Influence

58. **"Our examples are like seeds on a windy day, they spread far and wide."**

Kindness

**59. "Deal with the faults
of others
as gently
as with your own."
(Chinese)**

**60. "The man who
remembers others,
remembers also
his Creator."**

Knowledge

61. "Knowledge is like
a garden:
if it is not cultivated,
it cannot be harvested."
(Guinea)

62. "Knowledge is better
than riches."
(Cameroon)

Leadership

63. **"A good chief gives,
he does not take."
(Mohawk)**

Love

64. "Let your love be like the misty rain, coming softly, but flooding the river." (Liberia)

65. "Love is like a baby: it needs to be treated tenderly." (Zaire)

**66. "Love is like the sun, it warms you all over, can turn the darkest day bright, and life would be cold without it."
(Mr. "B")**

67. "When we understand the sun, our love will warm the earth." (Rosicrucian)

68. "Love is better than a whip."

Parents

69. **"A child without
a mother
is like a fish
in shallow water."**

70. **"One father is more
than a hundred
schoolmasters."
(English)**

71. **"A piece of iron can only become what the blacksmith says it should become."
(Mynamar)**

Patience

72. "Patience is bitter but its fruit is sweet." (French)

73. "The spider that knows what it will gain sits waiting patiently in its web. The praying mantis is never tired waiting all day."

74. **"Patience is power. With time and patience the mulberry leaf becomes silk." (Chinese)**

Persistence

75. "A little rain each day will fill the rivers to overflowing." (Liberia)

76. "It is little by little that a bird builds its nest."

Planning

77. "He who does not
look ahead
always remains behind."

78. "In his heart
a man may plan
his course
but God determines
his every step."
(from Moon Over
Morocco)

79. **"The palest ink is better than the best memory."**
(Chinese)

Practice

80. "Practice makes perfect." (English)

Praise

81. **"Praise the young
and they will blossom."
(Irish)**

Prayer

82. **"Pray indeed,
but get to work!"
(Mexican)**

Procrastination

83. "Never put off till tomorrow what may be done today."
(English)

84. "No time like the present."
(English)

85. "Procrastination is the thief of time."

86. "One of these days is none of these days." (English)

87. "It is not enough to run, one must start in time." (French)

88. "Tomorrow is often the busiest day of the week." (Spanish)

Regrets

89. "A man is not old
until his regrets
take the place
of his dreams."
(John Barrymore)

90. "Don't let yesterday
use up too much
of today."
(Cherokee)

Respect

91. **"When we show our respect for other living things, they respond with respect for us."**
(Arapaho)

Seeing

92. **"The mind is for seeing, the heart is for hearing."**
(Arabic)

Self-Awareness

**93. "You can outdistance
that which is
running after you,
but not what is
running inside you."
(Rwandan)**

**94. "He who looks outside,
dreams;
he who looks inside,
awakens."
(Carl Jung)**

Silence

95. **"A silent mouth
is melodious."
(Irish)**

Society

96. "A society grows great when old men plant trees whose shade they know they shall never sit in." (Greek)

Sowing and Reaping

97. "More grows
in the garden
than the gardener knows
he has sown."
(Spanish)

98. "One generation
plants the trees;
another gets the shade."
(Chinese)

Sorrow

99. "Sorrow is like rice in the store; if a basket full is removed everyday, it will come to an end at last."
(Somalia)

Success

100. "Everyone who is successful must have dreamed of something." (Maricopa)

Talking

**101. "To talk
without thinking
is to shoot
without aiming."
(English)**

**102. "One must talk little,
and listen much."
(Mauritania)**

103. **"The owl is the wisest of all birds because the more it sees, the less it talks."**

Teachers

104. **"A teacher is better than two books."**
(German)

Teaching

105. "If a drum is
not made,
it is the fault
of the master;
but if the drum is made
and is not beaten,
then that is the fault
of the boys."

106. "Too large a morsel
chokes the child."
(Mauritania)

107. "Advise and
counsel him;
if he does not listen,
let adversity teach him."

108. "Give a man a fish,
and he'll eat for a day.
Teach him how to fish
and he'll eat forever."
(Chinese)

109. **"To teach is to learn."
(Japanese)**

Thoughtfulness

110. "Thoughts and dreams are the foundation of our being."

111. "The habit of thinking is the habit of gaining strength."

112. "We are what our thinking makes us."

Time

113. "Yesterday
is but a dream,
tomorrow
is but a vision.
But today well lived
makes every yesterday
a dream of happiness,
and every tomorrow
a vision of hope.
Look well, therefore,
to this Day."
(Sanskrit)

Today

114. **"Today is the first day of the rest of your life."**

Tomorrow

115. **"Tomorrow is a new day." (English)**

Trials

116. **"The gem cannot be polished without friction, nor man perfected without trials." (Chinese)**

Unity

117. **"A single tree can not make a forest."**

Wisdom

**118. "A wise man
hears one word
and understands two."
(Yiddish)**

**119. "Seek wisdom,
not knowledge.
Knowledge is of the past,
wisdom is of the future."
(Lumbee)**

120. **"A wise man makes his own decisions, an ignorant man follows the public opinion."**
(Chinese)

For Your Students
(These are short quotes that you can
use specifically in the classroom
or at home.)

121. "Trouble rides
a fast horse."
(Italian)

122. "He who lies
with dogs
shall rise up with fleas."
(Latin)

**123.   "If you watch
your pot,
your food will not burn."
(Niger)**

**124. "You must
act as if
it is impossible
to fail."
(Ashanti)**

125. **"It takes two to make a quarrel." (Guinea)**

Teacher Quotes
(Things People Have Said)

126. "Those who educate children well are more to be honored than parents, for these only gave life, those the art of living well." (Aristotle)

127. "A teacher affects eternity: he can never tell where his influence stops." (Henry Adams)

128. "What nobler
employment,
or more valuable
to the state,
than that of the man
who instructs
the rising generation."
(Marcus Tullius Cicero)

129. "It is the supreme art
of the teacher
to awaken joy
in creative expression
and knowledge."
(Albert Einstein)

130. "Treat the students the way you would want to be treated."

131. "A gifted teacher is as rare as a gifted doctor, and makes far less money."

132. "No one
has yet fully realized
the wealth of sympathy,
kindness,
and generosity
hidden in the soul
of a child.
The effort of
every true education
should be to unlock
that treasure."
(Emma Golmam)

133. **"Kind words can be short and easy to speak, but their echoes are endless."
(Mother Teresa)**

134. **"It is not so much what is poured into the student, but what is planted that really counts."
(Unknown)**

135. **"One good teacher
in a lifetime
may sometimes change
a delinquent
into a solid citizen."
(Philip Wylie)**

136. "A hundred years
from now
it will not matter
what my bank account
was,
the sort of house
I lived in,
or the kind of car
I drove . . . .
but the world
may be different
because I was important
in the life of a child."
(Kathy Davis)

137. "He who dares
to teach
must never cease
to learn."

138. "The important thing
is not so much
that every child
should be taught,
as that every child
should be given
the wish to learn."
(John Lubbock)

139. "They may forget
what you said,
but they will never forget
how you made
them feel."

140. "The secret of teaching
is to appear
to have known
all your life
what you learned
this afternoon."

141. "The work can wait
while you show the child
the rainbow,
but the rainbow
won't wait
while you do the work."
(Patricia Clafford)

142. "I touch the future.
I teach."
(Christa McAuliffe)

143. **"To teach is to touch lives forever."**

144. **"A good teacher is like a candle - it consumes itself to light the way for others."**

145. **"The best teachers teach from the heart, not from the book."**

146. "To me,
education is a
leading out
of what is already there
in the pupil's soul."
(Muriel Spark)

147. "Teachers who inspire
know that teaching
is like cultivating
a garden,
and those who would have
nothing to do with thorns
must never attempt
to gather flowers."
(Author Unknown)

148. "The teacher
who is indeed wise
does not bid you
to enter the house
of his wisdom
but rather leads you
to the threshold
of your mind."
(Kahlil Gibran)

149. "Teaching kids to count
is fine,
but teaching them
what counts
is best."
(Bob Talbert)

150. "The mediocre teacher tells.
The good teacher explains.
The superior teacher demonstrates.
The great teacher inspires."
(William Ward)

151. **"Teacher: The child's third parent." (Hyman Berston)**

152. **"We can learn many things from children... like how much patience we have."**

153. "It must be remembered
that the purpose of
education is not
to fill the minds
of students with facts...
it is to teach them
to think,
if that is possible,
and always to think
for themselves."
(Robert Hutchins)

154. "Teaching should be full of ideas instead of stuffed with facts."

155. "We cannot hold a torch to light another's path without brightening our own." (Ben Sweetland)

156. "A child miseducated is a child lost." (John F. Kennedy)

157. **"A forest is in an acorn."**

I Couldn't Forget-Me-Nots
(Teachers and Others)

I would like to send out a special thanks to all of the teachers that invited me as a guest teacher in their classrooms. I learned so much and I thank you.

To the principals, assistant principals and administrators that gave me help and advice, thank you. To all of the secretaries and office workers that always shared a smile and welcomed me when I came to your schools, I appreciate it. Extra special thanks to the food services and cafeteria workers that kept me fed and full, I appreciate your work.

Special recognition goes outs to my team members at Woodland Middle School (East Point, GA): Ms. Fletcher, Mrs. Zelner, Mr. Potts, Mr. Thomas, Mrs. Cumberlander. Thank you for showing me why Special Education is special; the teachers. I appreciate all of your help and support. Mr. Bradley, Mr. Wright, Mr. Butler, Ms. Randolph, Dr. Ware, Mr. Harden, Dr. Brown, and everyone else at Woodland MS (East Point). Thank you all.

To Dr. Miller, Mrs. Cainion, and all of the teachers and staff at Mary Bethune ES. Every one at Connally ES (APS) and Mr. Underdue (Brown MS). Thank you for your support.

To Mr. Sims, Mr. Harden, and everyone else at Paul D. West MS (East Point, GA), thank you all. *"**Go Panthers!**"*

All of the teachers, administrators, and staff at College Park ES, Conley Hills ES, Crossroads SC, Hapeville ES, Hamilton Holmes ES, Oak Knoll ES, Parklane ES, Tri-Cities HS, Harriet Tubman ES, Banneker HS, Heritage ES, Love Nolan ES, Mount Olive ES, Ronald McNair MS, and all of the other schools in South Fulton County.

Thank you also to Dr. Lynch, Linda Coffey, and Nancy O'Barr.

I Couldn't Forget-Me-Nots (Part 2)
(Family and Others)

To my family and friends: You have given me the love and support that I needed in order to demand more from myself.

In special remembrance of my father, Moses Butts.

To my mother, my brother Jonathan, my Aunt Mary and Uncle Wayne, my Aunt Darline and Uncle Bobby, my Aunt Betty and Uncle Leroy, my Uncle Frank, my Aunt Liz and Uncle Warren, my Uncle William Henry, my Aunt Loretha and Uncle Boisy. Nelson and Loraine Wyart and family. The entire Head family, and the entire Scruggs family. The Butts family. And to all of my cousins, nieces, nephews, and extended family. I love you all.

To Mrs. Dunn, my first grade teacher. Mrs. Lespier (Mays) my second grade teacher. Mrs. Bennie, my third grade teacher. Mr. Francis. Ms. Stevenson, my fourth grade teacher. Mrs. Harris (Fulton). Mrs. Hanna. Ms. Joseph. Mr. And Mrs. Humphrey. Mrs. Dean. Mrs. Ross and Mrs. Byrd my choir directors. Mr. Semande. Mrs. Inman. Mrs. Brise. Mrs. Ruff. Mrs. McCall. Mrs. Rodriguez. Ms. Barnes. Mrs. Taylor. Mrs. Doggette. Mrs. Dorsey. Ms. Hodge. Ms. Bowles. Mrs. Alexander. Mrs. Munroe. Thank you all.

To the men that stood for something and showed young boys examples of what real men are. Mr. Miller. Mr. Ryan. Mr. Brise. Mr. Anderson "Andy Sandy" Sandiford (thank you for giving me a love of the English language and for teaching me how to think critically). Mr. Clifford LaGuerre (your example has taught me more than I can express in words). To Mr. Frost, the greatest band teacher in the world (my trumpet and band teacher). Mr. Jobson (I look back and I'm amazed at your dedication and work ethic). Mr. Hayward.

Special thanks to Mr. Armstrong, my AmeriCorps family, and everyone at Hands on Atlanta. ***Keep caring!***

I Couldn't Forget-Me-Nots (Part 2)
(Family and Others) (cont'd)

To my college Professors and teachers at Oakwood: Mrs. Tucker (my mentor, adviser, and college mom. You saw something that has taken me a long time to discover and develop. I'm finally coming into my own). Mr. Tucker (a successful Christian businessman). Mrs. Gunn. Mr. Green. Mr. Samson. Pastor E.E. Cleveland (an intellectual, historical, and spiritual giant). Mr. Bartholomew (your words continue to encourage me). Officer M. Kirby. Minneola Dixon. Thank you all.

To the members of Gamma Psi Gamma and Beta Alpha Theta. There's not enough room here for me to thank all of you. Just know that you are all in my heart. We are family. (OoooohOooooh!) (I Love Sapphires!)

To the Northside SDA Church in Miami Florida. Pastor Denton Rhone at the Belvedere SDA Church (Decatur, Georgia). Lydia and Monet Floyd, the entire Floyd family, and the Boulevard SDA Church (Atlanta). Sister Storne, Charles, Renita, Tyrone, Carl, Darlene, and to all of the family, thank you for treating me like family. The Decatur SDA Church (Decatur, Georgia). To Pastor Michael Ross and everyone at the Dixie Seventh-Day Adventist Church. Extra special thanks to Elder Calvin Hosendolph for helping me get my computer up and working again...this is what I needed it for...thank you. To Brother and Sister Joseph, and Yul Joseph and family.

Special thanks to: Mark, Dave, and Demond for looking out for me. Glenn Sun, Kyle Gabriel, Leroy Dantzler, Desmond Smith (thank you again!), Big Country and family, Odiri Ukuedojor ("Nigeria's finest"), Dee Brown, Jason Youngblood and family, Basil Blake, Barrington Dames, Joey Dillon, Dr. James Mosley III, Famous Murray Jr. and family, Mike Smith and family, W. Nate Simons and family. Kamal Tyson and Harold Harris. Thank you all! And to Mr. George Andrews thank you for listening.

About the Author

Joseph Butts is an entrepreneur and small business owner living in the Atlanta Georgia metropolitan area. He has worked as a substitute teacher in the Fulton County School System where he developed a love for teaching and a *"lovethemevenwhentheygetonyourlastnerve"* love for students.

He has earned his *"stripes"* by working in some of the most challenging classrooms outside of the "state pen". And he has been officially christened as "Mr. B." by adoring (and sometimes not-so-adoring) students across Fulton county Georgia.

He says, **"There's a lot that you can learn about a teacher just from how their students act when the teacher is away. There's the *'party-over-here-this-may-be-the-only-time-that-we-get-to-show-out'* attitude. The *'please-oh-please-oh-please-take-us-with-you-when-you-leave'* attitude. And the, *'don't-take-it-personally-we-act-like-this-every-day'* experience. But regardless of what happens, I usually always end up having a good day with the students."**

He holds a Bachelors of Science degree in Business Management and would maybe possibly someday eventually like to work as a full-time Language Arts or Business Education teacher.

This book is his way of giving back.

Order Form

We offer special discounts for schools and bulk orders of five or more. To find out more information email us at: **books@applehearts.com.**

For information on seminars, speaking engagements and *"Encouragement workshops"* contact us at: **speaking@applehearts.com.**

For more information on additional books and resources visit us at: **www.applehearts.com**

To order by mail please complete the order form below and send check or money order to:

Apple Hearts Media
Atlanta, GA

When Nobody Brings You An Apple

Over 101 Proverbs and Quotes To Encourage and Inspire Your Favorite Teachers, Principals, Support Staff, and School Administrators

Name: _____

Address:_____

City:_____ State:_____

Zip:_____ Phone (w/ area code):_____

Number of copies:_____@ $12.97 per copy =Total
$_____

For shipping and handling please add $3.97 for the first book and $2.97 for each additional book.

Total enclosed: $_____

Email books@applehearts.com for special discounts on 5 or more

Coloring Sheet

Color the apple and then give it to yourself...
"when nobody brings you an apple"